UKULELE

SAM SMITH
IN THE LONELY HOUR

ISBN 978-1-4950-2971-4

HAL•LEONARD®
CORPORATION
7777 W. BLUEMOUND RD. P.O. BOX 13819 MILWAUKEE, WI 53213

Visit Hal Leonard Online at
www.halleonard.com

Money on My Mind

Words and Music by Sam Smith and Benjamin Ross Ash

mind.   No   mon - ey   on   my   mind,   no   mon - ey   on   my   mind.

1. No,   I   have   no   mon - ey   on   my   mind. _____   When the   **2.** mind, _____   just _

Interlude

love.

1., 2.   **3.**

D.S. al Coda

Coda

love.   I   do   it   for   the   love.

Outro

Good Thing

Words and Music by Sam Smith and Eg White

to stay with you would be wrong. _____ Too much of a good _
to stay with you would be wrong. _____ Too much of a good _
and I got noth-ing at all. _____ Too much of a good _

_____ thing _ won't be good an - y - more. ___
_____ thing _ won't be good an - y - more. ___
_____ thing _ is - n't good and you know. ___

Watch where I tread _____ be - fore I _____ fall.
Watch where I tread _____ be - fore I _____
I watch where I walk _____ be - fore I _____

fall.

D.S. al Coda

fall.

To Coda

Coda

fall. Be - fore I fall.

Stay with Me

Words and Music by Sam Smith, James Napier, William Edward Phillips, Tom Petty and Jeff Lynne

Outro-Chorus

Oh, won't you ___ stay ___ with me? ___

___ 'Cause you're ___ all ___ I ___ need. ___

___ This ain't ___ love, it's clear ___ to see. ___

___ But, dar-ling, ___ stay ___ with me. ___

1.   2.

___ Oh, won't you ___

Leave Your Lover

Words and Music by Sam Smith and Simon Aldred

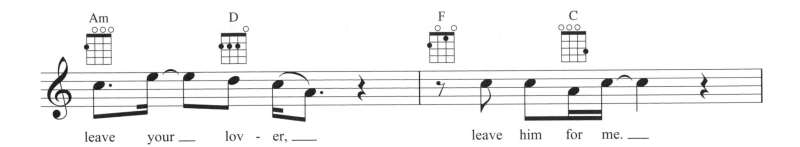

leave your ___ lov - er, ___   leave him for me. ___

Leave your ___ lov - er, ___   leave him for me. ___

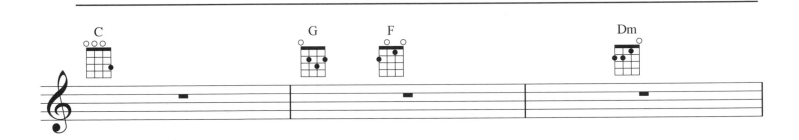

leave him for me. ___

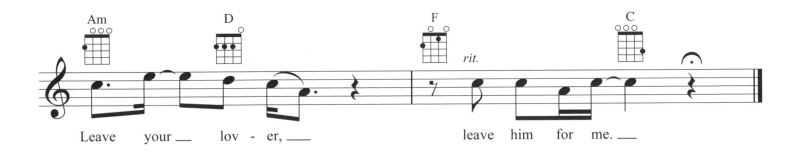

Leave your ___ lov - er, ___   leave him for me. ___

I'm Not the Only One

Words and Music by Sam Smith and James Napier

Chorus

You say I'm cra-zy ____ 'cause you don't think I know what you've done. ____ But when you call ____ me ____ ba-by, ____ I know I'm not the on-ly one. ____

Bridge

I have loved you for man-y years.

May-be I am just not e-nough. ____ You've made me real-ize my deep-est fear by ly-ing and tear-ing us up. ____ You

I've Told You Now

Words and Music by Sam Smith and Eg White

Pre-Chorus

Still, I re - frain __ from talk - ing at you, talk - ing on. You

Chorus

know me well; __ I don't ex - plain. __ But what the hell? __

Why do you think I come 'round here on my free will, ___

wast - ing all my pre - cious time? __ Oh, the truth spills out, __

_____ and, oh, _____ oh, I, __

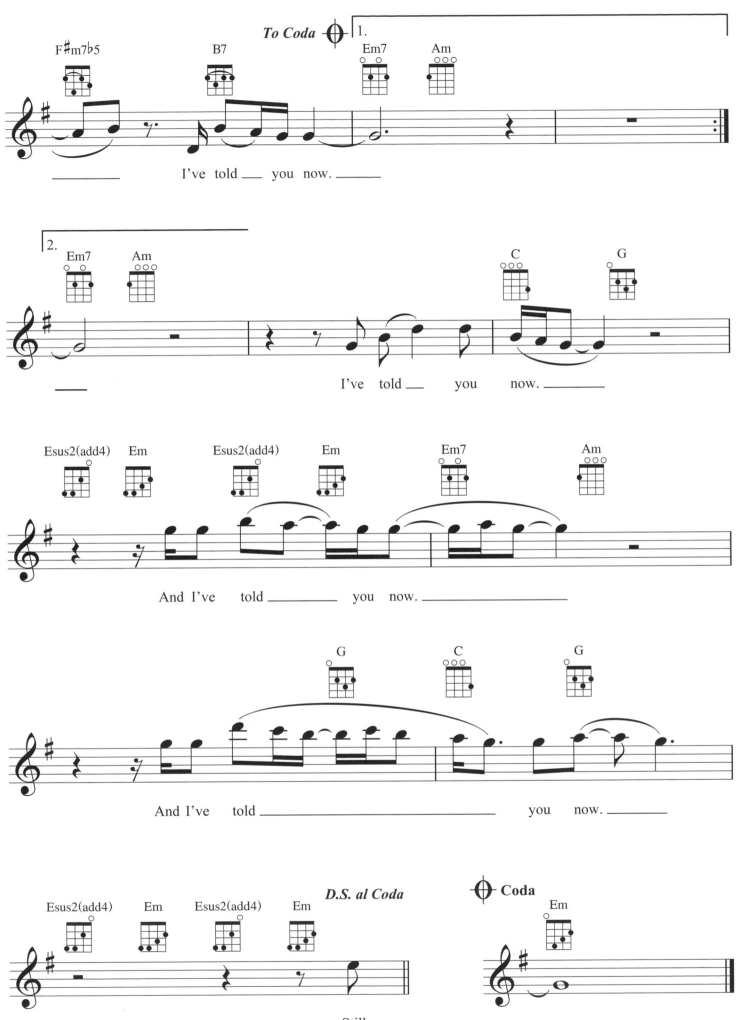

Like I Can

Words and Music by Sam Smith and Matt Prime

glance. He could be a tro - phy of a
stance. May - be he's a man - tra, keeps your

one - night stand. ___ He could have your hu - mor, _____ but I
mind en - tranced. __ He could be the si - lence _____ in this

don't un - der - stand, _____ 'cause) he'll nev - er love you like I
may - hem, __ but then a - gain,)

𝄋 Chorus

can, can, can. Why are you __ look - ing __ down

all the wrong roads ___ when mine __ is the heart and the

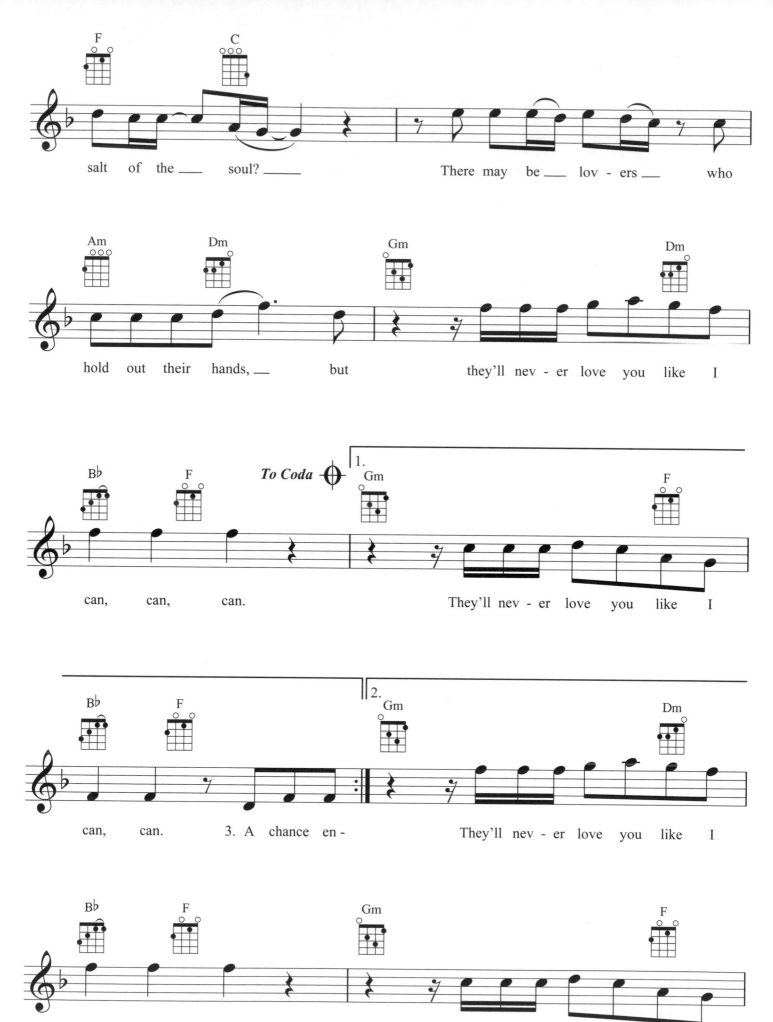

salt   of the ___ soul? ____

There may be ___ lov - ers ___   who

hold   out their hands, ___   but

they'll nev - er love you like   I

To Coda 1.

can,   can,   can.

They'll nev - er love you like   I

2.

can,   can.   3. A   chance en -

They'll nev - er love you like   I

can,   can,   can.

They'll nev - er love you like   I

Life Support

Words and Music by Sam Smith and Benjamin Ross Ash

be - cause I built this bed for two.

I'm just hang - ing on your an - swer. _____

I've built this bed for me and you.

Chorus

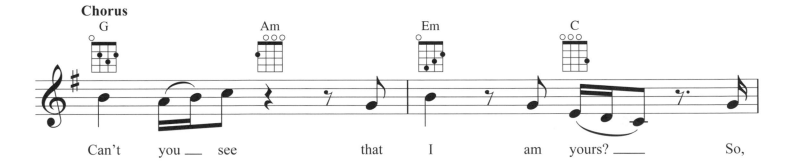

Can't you _ see that I am yours? _____ So,

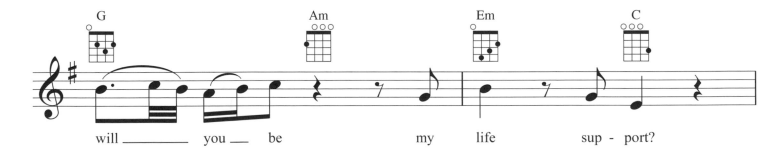

will _____ you _ be my life sup - port?

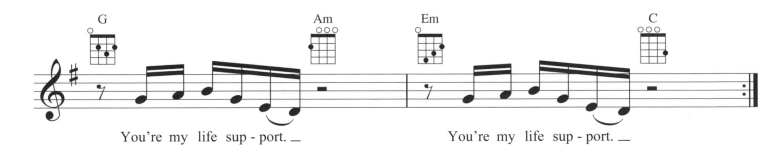

You're my life sup - port. _ You're my life sup - port. _

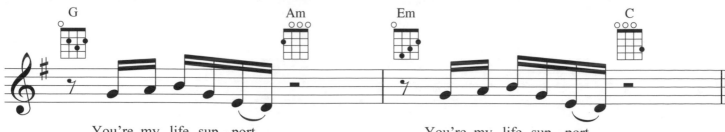

You're my life sup - port. __   You're my life sup - port. __

Interlude

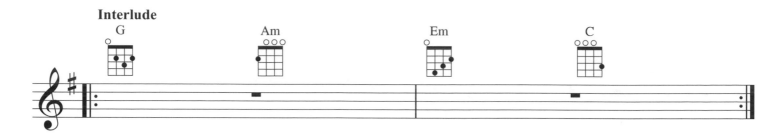

Outro-Chorus

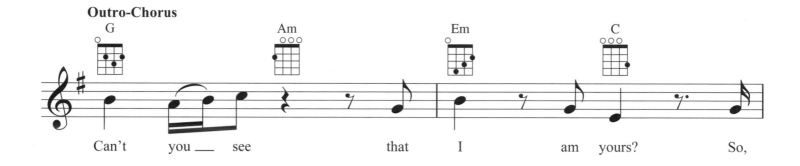

Can't you __ see   that   I   am yours?   So,

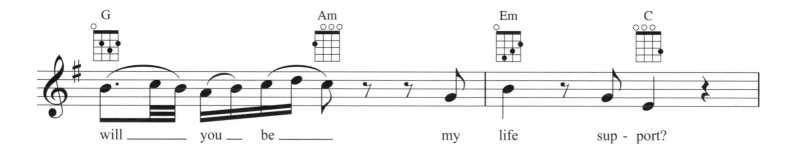

will _____ you __ be _____   my life sup - port?

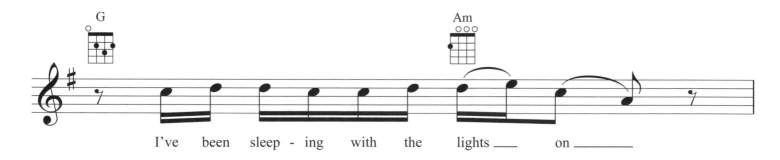

I've been sleep - ing with the lights __ on _____

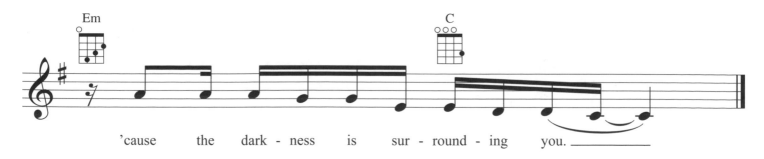

'cause the dark - ness is sur - round - ing you. _____

Not in That Way

Words and Music by Sam Smith and Fraser T. Smith

Bridge

fool.   When you're   not there, _____

_____   I   find   my - self   sing - ing   the   blues.   Can't   bear,

can't   face _____   the   truth. _____   You _____   will

Coda

love   you,   but   not   in   that   way."   You'd   say,   "I'm

sor - ry;   be - lieve   me,   I   love   you,   but   not   in   that   way."

Lay Me Down

Words and Music by Sam Smith, James Napier and Elvin Smith

1. Yes, I do, I be - lieve that one day I will be where I was, right there, right next to you. ____ And it's hard; the days just seem so dark. The moon and the stars are noth-ing with-out you. Your touch, your skin; where do I be-gin? No words can ex-plain the way I'm miss-ing you. ____

_____ De-ny this emp-ti-ness, this hole that I'm in - side. These tears, they tell their own sto - ry. You

Pre-Chorus

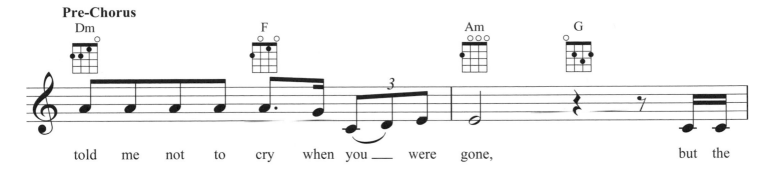

told me not to cry when you ___ were gone, but the

feel- ing's o - ver-whelm - ing; it's much too _____ strong. ___ Can

Chorus

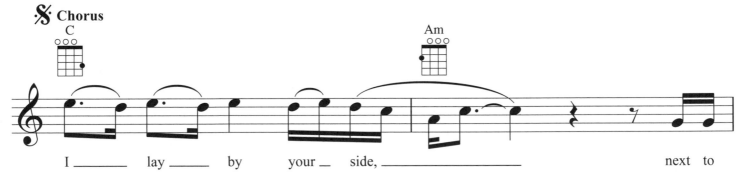

I _____ lay _____ by your _ side, _____ next to

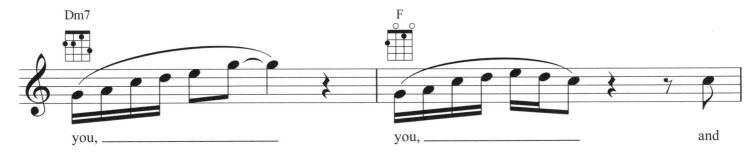

you, _____ you, _____ and

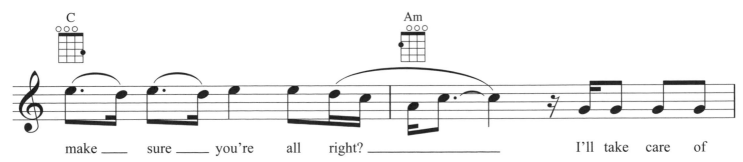

make ___ sure ___ you're all right? _____ I'll take care of

you. _____ I don't want to be here if I can't be with you _

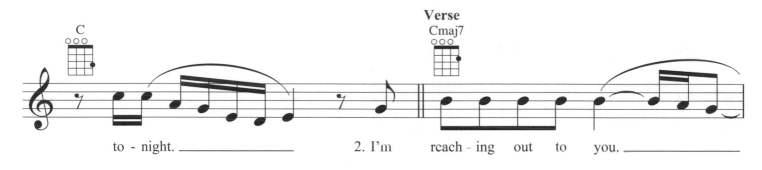

Verse

to - night. _____ 2. I'm reach - ing out to you. _____

_____ Can you hear _ my _ call? _____ This

hurt that I've been through, _____ I'm miss - ing you, miss - ing you like

D.S. al Coda

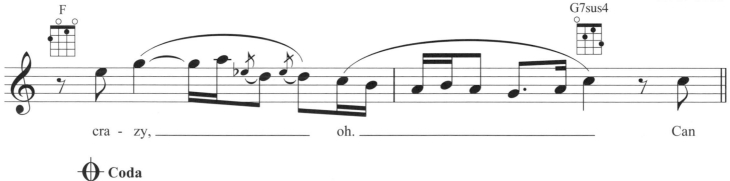

cra - zy, _____ oh. _____ Can

Coda
Bridge

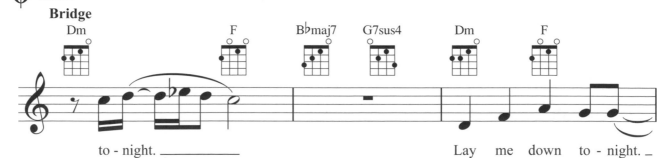

to - night. _____ Lay me down to - night. _

Restart

Words and Music by Sam Smith and Zane Lowe

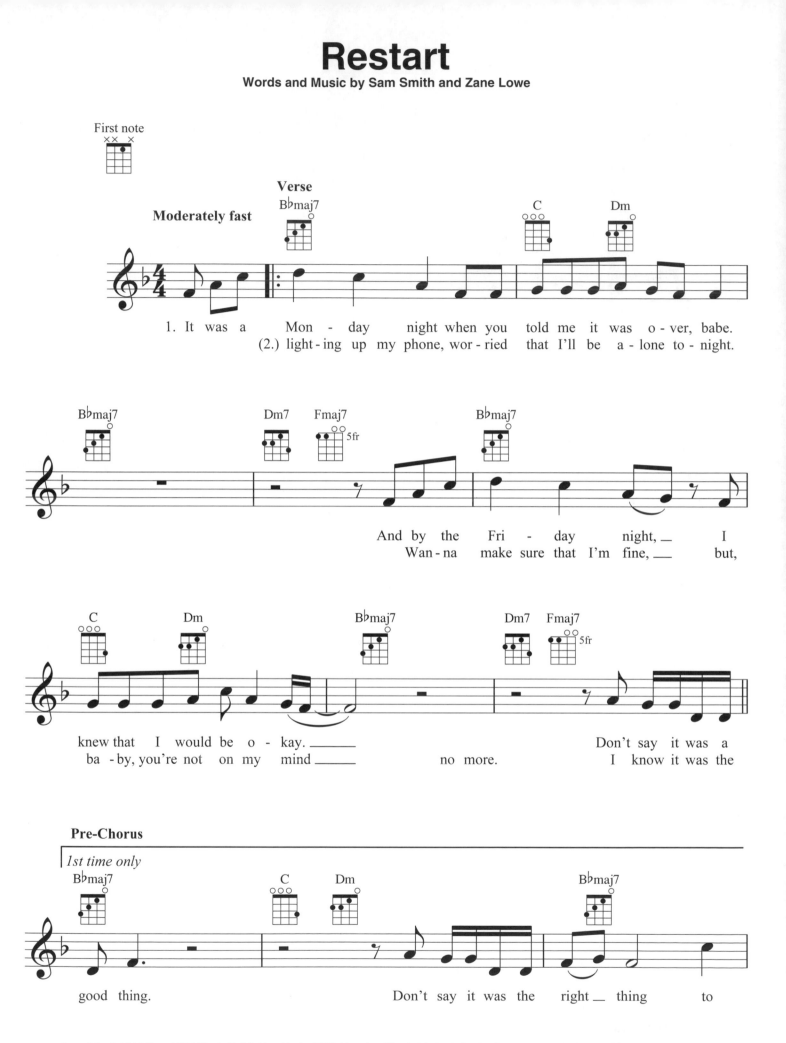

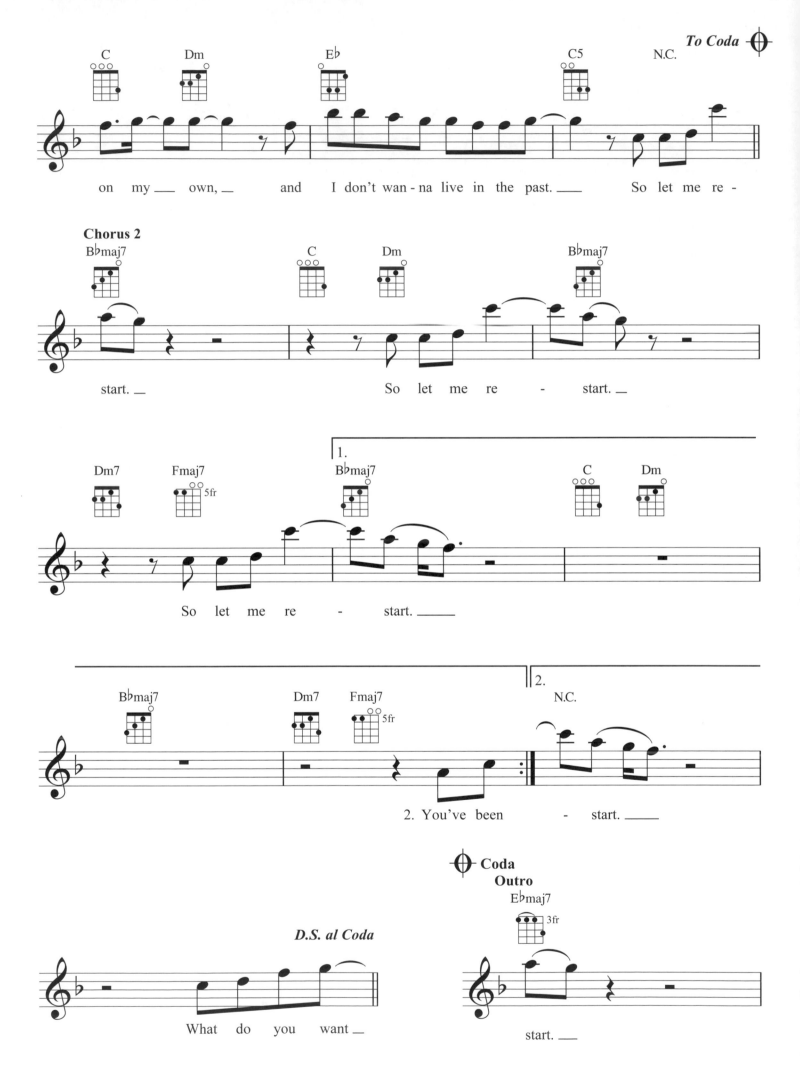

La La La

Words and Music by Al Hakam El Kaubaisy, James Murray, Mustafa Omer, Sam Smith, Shahid Khan, James Napier, Jonnie Coffer and Frobisher Mbabazi

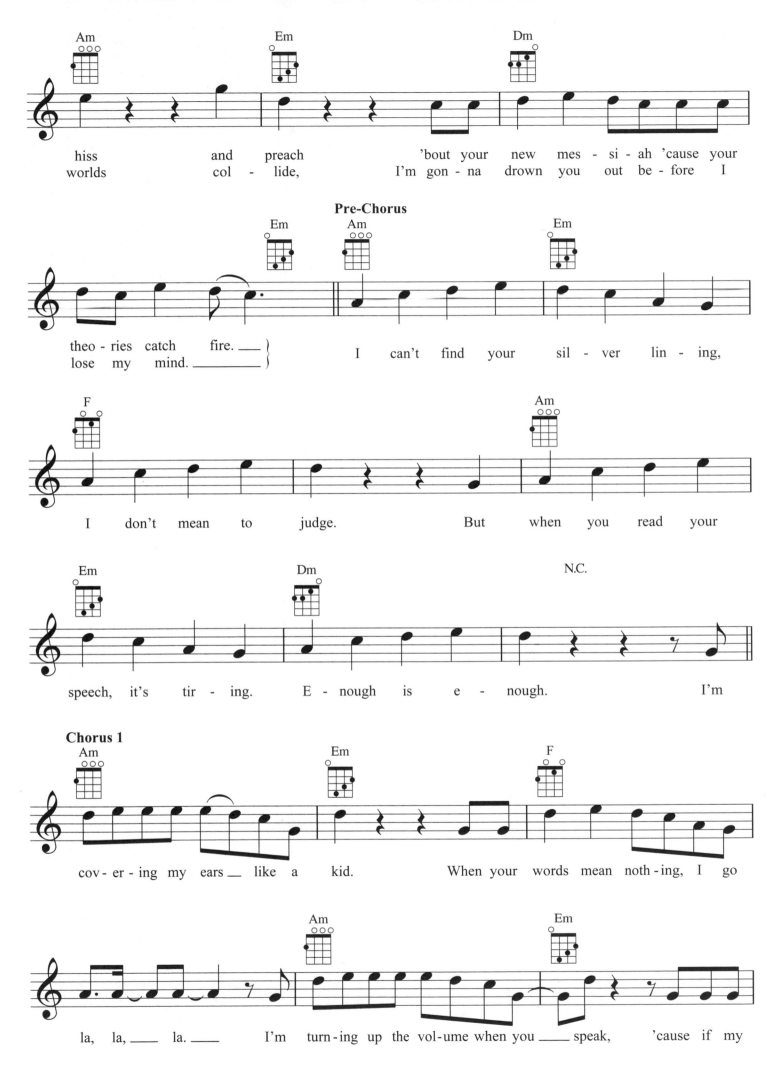

Chorus 1

na, na, la, la, la, la, la. Do-hey-ee, oh, __ do-hey.)   I'm cov-er-ing my ears __ like a

kid.   When your words mean noth-ing, I go la, la, __ la. __ I'm

turn-ing up the vol-ume when you __ speak,   'cause if my heart can't stop it,   I'll

Outro-Chorus 2

find a way to block it. I go... (Na, na, la, la, la, la, la, na, na, na, na, na. La, la,

na, na, la, la, la, la, la, na, na, na, na, na. La, la, na, na, la, la, la, la, la,

na, na, na, na, na. La, la, na, na, la, la, la, la, la. Do-hey-ee, oh, __ do-hey.)

Make It to Me

Words and Music by Sam Smith, James Napier and Howard Lawrence

dis - tant stran - ger ___ that I will com - plete. ___ I

know you're out ___ there; we're meant to be. ___ So,

keep your head ___ up ___ and make it to me, ___

___ and make it to me. ___

1.

2.
Make it to me. ___

Make it to me. ___

Latch

Words and Music by Guy Lawrence, Howard Lawrence, James Napier and Sam Smith

my em - brace. I'm latch - ing on ___ to you. ___

Outro-Chorus

Now I've got ___ you in my space. I won't let go of you. ___

___ Got you shack - led in my em - brace. I'm

latch - ing on ___ to you. ___ I'm

latch - ing on _____ to you. _____